Blink, Blink, Clop, Clop: Why Do We Do Things We Can't Stop?

An OCD Storybook

by E. Katia Moritz, Ph.D., & Jennifer Jablonsky

Illustrations by Rick Geary

Childswork Childsplay

Secaucus, New Jersey

Acknowledgements

With many thanks to Robert Rubenstein, Whitney Roban, and Karen Kuflik for helping to shape this manuscript. Special thanks for Robert for his dedication, love, and support of my work.

©1998 Childswork/Childsplay, LLC, a subsidiary of Genesis Direct, Inc.,
100 Plaza Drive, Secaucus, NJ 07094. 1-800-962-1141. All rights reserved.

Printed in the United States of America
8 7 6 5 4 3 2 1
ISBN# 1-882732-72-3

Cover and book design by Karin Batten

There are many challenges when dealing with OCD in children. Parents and professionals are always searching for the best way to help. A common question is whether or not the child should "know "about the OCD. The answer to this question may be found by talking to the children themselves.

Children suffering from OCD generally perceive that something is "wrong" with them but don't know what it is. They commonly make assumptions such as "I may be crazy" or "I am a weird kid." Left to themselves to understand this complicated condition, they may begin to feel blame, guilt, isolation, and depression.

Not knowing or understanding OCD can also make it very difficult to obtain positive results with the treatment. Aside from the pharmacological treatment, OCD requires the child to assume an active role. This relationship between the OCD and the child can almost be compared to a daily battle between listening or not listening, resisting or giving in.

This book was written to give children, parents, and professionals the beginning tools to enter this treatment arena. In this story, O.C. Flea symbolizes that little voice that children sometimes refer to when talking about OCD. We hope that through the portrayal of the animals in the story, the child will set out on an important journey to understanding his or her symptoms.

Some of the animals' symptoms may never have been experienced by the child you are treating. However, these may be used in a discussion to help the child understand the irrational nature of OCD, which is often easier to see in the symptoms of others.

Even though there is no OCD flea, we wish that, like the O. C. Flea, OCD could become a little "thing" that does not stop kids from being happy and getting everything they deserve in life.

♣ **To the brave little ones** ♣

Life on Farmer Brown's farm seemed peaceful and perfect. The crops were watered and the fields were ploughed. The animals were well fed and well cared for.

But for some of the animals on the farm, life wasn't so perfect or peaceful. These animals were very unhappy. They spent most of their days worrying. Their thoughts were troubled. They did odd things over and over again. Their strange behavior made them feel left out and lonely. And they did all this because of an unpleasant fellow named O. C. Flea. O. C. Flea was just a tiny bug, but he made much bigger animals (whose size he envied!) think and do things that made them feel miserable!

For example, at the chicken coop, every day at lunch time, Farmer Brown would reach into his dusty silver bucket and throw handfuls of feed to the chickens. The chickens would happily peck at the chicken feed that was scattered on the ground—all except for Henrietta, who would stand off to the side and listen to the pesky, droning voice of O. C. Flea.

"I'm telling you," O. C. Flea warned. "If you don't arrange that row of feed into a nice, straight line, Farmer Brown's going to come and plow right over your chicken coop, and you and all of your feathered friends will be crushed! And it will be all your fault!"

"It's still a little crooked," Henrietta exclaimed helplessly, as she tried to line up her feed. She would move the little grains up and down, to the right and left, but the line was never straight enough to satisfy O. C. Flea. In fact, Henrietta spent so much time on this impossible task that she rarely got to eat her lunch.

Late in the afternoon, all the chickens would settle down into soft piles of straw to lay their eggs. Most of the chickens would finish very quickly, then leave to play Ring Around the Chicken Coop, Hide 'n Seek, or other games. Not Henrietta. Every time she left her pile of straw, she would hear O. C. Flea say, "Are you *sure* you laid your egg? You'd better go back and check!"

Henrietta would say to herself, "Maybe I just *think* I laid my eggs. What if I thought I did it, but I really didn't?" These thoughts would make her worry so much that she would check again and again to see if her eggs were in the hay, even though, deep down, she knew that she had laid them. "What if I thought I saw my eggs there, but I really didn't? I should look again, and this will be the last time!" But it never was.

The more Henrietta listened to O. C. Flea, the stranger she became. Her new thing to do before going to bed was to try to fluff out her feathers so they looked perfectly symmetrical. She'd work at it for hours, way past her bedtime. "I know it's silly," Henrietta cried. "When I fall asleep my feathers will get all messed up. I just can't help it! They have to look right, or I won't sleep!"

At cow-milking time, the barn was usually pretty quiet, except for the SPLAT, SPLAT sound of milk squirting into buckets and the occasional clank of a cowbell.

"So, my milk will go from the bucket to the machine, into the bottle, into boxes, onto a truck, to the supermarket, to somebody's car, into the kitchen, into a glass, and finally into someone's tummy, right?" Daisy asked her friend Maybelle.

"Yes! Yes!" Maybelle replied, exhausted. "Holy cow! I've already told you this a million times. Isn't that enough?"

"Ask again," prodded O. C. Flea. "She may not have understood exactly what you were asking. Are you sure she said yes? She might have said no."

For the next few hours, Daisy would ask the same questions over and over. "Maybelle, what if my milk sits in the truck too long and spoils, and then somebody drinks it and gets sick? What if the bottle is dirty and my milk tastes bad? What if. . . "For mooing out loud!" Maybelle would shriek. "Stop asking these silly questions and just let the farmer milk you already!"

"Maybelle" Daisy would continue. "I can't let him milk me. I think I have a temperature. I might be sick! Can you check?"

After rubbing her nose against Daisy's for about the fifth time that day, Maybelle assured her, "No, Daisy. You don't have a fever." But Daisy was still not quite sure.

And just when everybody thought Daisy's situation couldn't get any worse, O. C. Flea told her, "Daisy, I think you're drooling! Into the milk!"

"No, I'm not," she answered. But she wiped her mouth just to be sure.

"Well, you'd better start wiping your mouth all the time," said O. C. Flea. "You never know when some of your drool might get into your milk, and that would be really, really bad!"

At first, Daisy didn't believe O. C. Flea. But eventually, O. C. Flea convinced her that it was possible for someone to drool and not know it. And once again she listened. She started to wipe her mouth all the time, especially after she had a drink, just to be sure she wasn't drooling

Many of the other cows, including Maybelle, were very sad about what was happening to Daisy. They weren't sure how to act or reply when Daisy asked them questions. "I don't understand," said Maybelle to another cow. "It seems the more we answer her questions, the worse she gets. I'm so tired of answering her questions, but at the same time, I feel bad for her. I know she doesn't mean to be annoying. It seems like she just can't help it."

The pig pen was a lively place, where the pigs were always wrestling in the cool mud or slinging it, making angels in the mud, or having slop-eating contests.

But Snort, the smartest pig in the pig pen, never joined the others. Like Daisy and Henrietta, he couldn't ignore the malicious words of O. C. Flea. The fact that Snort was so smart only made the other pigs wonder even more why Snort listened to O. C. Flea.

"Better wash again," O. C. Flea would tell him. "I still see a few specs of mud left. It's still not clean enough." Snort spent a lot of time by himself showering by the water pump while the other pigs romped in the mud. In fact, he washed himself so often that he nearly washed the pink off his skin! The constant spray of water and scrubbing made his hooves dry and rough as sandpaper.

WASHING
1. HEAD
2. TUMMY
3. LEGS
4. HOOVES
5. START AGAIN

Then one day, to make matters worse, O. C. Flea warned Snort, "If I were you, I'd start saying "Ahem" before you oink—you know, like you're clearing your throat. If you don't, you're going to get sick and die!"

"You're making that up," Snort insisted. "How can making a sound like that protect me?"

"I wouldn't take any chances," replied O. C. Flea.

After that, Snort could often be heard saying "Ahem, oink" while he was showering.

"Hey, Soapy," the other pigs would tease. "You look more like a big marshmallow than a pig."

"And who ever heard of a pig that coughs before he oinks, like you do?" one of the other pigs shouted.

Snort felt miserable. He wished he could play in the mud and be like the other pigs. But he felt he had to listen to O. C. Flea.

At the stable, there was a constant CLOP, CLOP, CLOP noise coming from the horses' stalls.

"There goes Biscuit again," complained Trotter, the pony whose stall was next to Biscuit's. "He disturbs the whole barn on account of that mean old O. C. Flea."

CLOP, CLOP, CLOP! "Why can't I stop tapping my foot?" came the sad voice from Biscuit's stall. "Not only do I have to tap, but I have to do it in just the right pattern! First the right hoof, then the left, then the right three times, then the left three times. . . I feel really stupid!" Biscuit said.

"Stop if you want," said O. C. Flea. "But don't come crying to me if the farmer slips off your saddle and breaks his neck when he's riding you. You know that the only way to prevent this is by tapping your hooves."

"Oh, my, I can't let that happen," said Biscuit. "I guess I'll keep doing it, even though it is silly."

"And while you're at it, you'd better blink your eyes, too, in the same pattern—just to be really sure there are no accidents." So poor Biscuit did. BLINK, BLINK, CLOP, CLOP, BLINK, BLINK, CLOP, CLOP.

Sometimes O. C. Flea would tell Trotter to stomp and blink, but Trotter wouldn't listen. "Get out of here!" Trotter would say. "You're full of baloney. You can't make things happen or not happen by doing those silly things."

"Why take the chance? Why not just do them?" O. C. Flea continued.

"I know what you're up to," Trotter said. "But it won't work with me. My answer is NO!"

This guy is no easy catch, thought O. C. Flea. *I'd better find someone else.*

Trotter tried to convince Biscuit to ignore O. C. Flea the way he did. But Biscuit only said, "I know I should, but I can't help it. It's too scary. And now you've made me lose track of my counting. I'll have to start all over again!" Biscuit turned away and continued to stomp and blink.

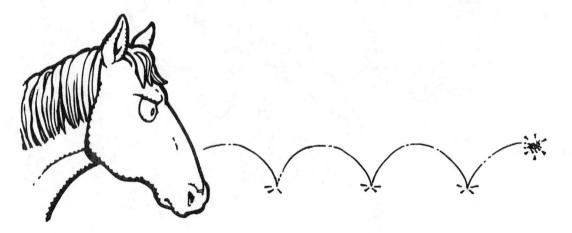

Farmer Brown couldn't understand why Biscuit had been acting so strange of late. He tried giving him carrots and sugar cubes to take his mind off whatever was disturbing him. They didn't help. So he decided to take Biscuit for a ride, hoping the fresh air would settle him down. But Biscuit stomped and blinked so often, he kept stumbling. So he slowed down to a turtle's pace, and the frustrated farmer finally brought him back to the barn.

Trotter sought out Hoot, the barn owl, for help. He had heard that owls were known for their wisdom. Hoot was just rising from his long afternoon nap.

"Hoot," he asked the owl, "why do some animals—like Biscuit—listen to O. C. Flea, while others don't?"

"The animals that listen to O. C. Flea are not really very different from the others. They are just more sensitive," said Hoot. "Their parents may be more sensitive, too, which is where they get it from."

"Sensitive?"

"Yes. It's like in springtime, when pollen from the flowers is in the air. Everyone gets pollen in their noses, but it makes some of us sneeze. It's the same way with O. C. Flea. All the animals hear the messages he sends. Some listen and some don't."

"What would happen to Biscuit if he stopped following O. C.'s rules?"

"Believe it or not, nothing. He would feel bad at first, but then the bad feeling would go away, and he would realize that he could ignore the flea and come to no harm."

"So, if something happened to stop Biscuit from doing the things he does, he might get better?"

"Yes," said the owl and flew off to hunt up some dinner.

One morning, the animals awoke to the loud rumble of thunder and the flash of lightning. A really big storm was coming! The winds, as though gone wild, whistled through the fields and trees. Thick black clouds hung over the farm, and large flocks of squawking birds sailed across the sky to escape the oncoming storm.

In the chicken coop, Henrietta was jumping around nervously. "The **wind is** swirling around all the feed!" she cried out frantically. "How am **I going** to keep it straight and lined up?"

The wind was also causing all the eggs to roll together in the straw. Nobody could tell whose egg was whose. "I don't know which is my egg," Henrietta raced around desperately. "What if I didn't lay an egg? I can't check now!"

As the hours passed, the winds grew even stronger. Henrietta's feathers all stuck out in crazy directions. "I look like a mess!" she cried. "I just know the farmer is going to come over here with his big tractor and crush us all!" She was trembling with fear.

From the big black sky, buckets of rain began to fall. Water leaked through the old, cracked roof of the barn. Daisy panicked. "Maybelle," she shouted, "what if water gets in our milk?" What if the pails topple over and the milk all spills out? I think I'm getting sick! Can you check to see if I have a temperature?" But the wind was loud, and Maybelle was busy trying to calm the young calves.

Daisy noticed that the other side of the barn was dry and out of the wind. She knew it would be best for her to carry the buckets there. "But what if I drool into them?" she thought. She decided that she would do it anyway. It was the only hope for saving the milk.

Over at the pig pen, the pigs were enjoying the sea of mud created by the heavy rains. They decided to have a contest to see who could get the muddiest.

Snort tried to wash off the mud that the wind and rain splashed on him. "Yuck!" he said. "This is gross!" But he couldn't get clean.

Desperate, Snort decided to stand on a pile of wet straw across the pen. But when he began to tiptoe through the mud to get there, he slipped and fell flat on his belly. He was covered in mud! He tried to stand up so he could wash off, but he soon lost his footing again and fell. There wasn't a clean spot on him!

The other pigs saw Snort covered in filth and could hardly **believe** their eyes. "I think we have the winner of the mud contest," **shouted** one of the other pigs, who didn't realize that Snort had gotten **dirty by** accident. All the pigs danced around Snort and played tag, and **Snort** forgot his troubles for a few moments and joined in the game. He **even** forgot to do his "Ahem" before he oinked in pleasure.

That night, though Snort felt very uncomfortable, he decided to **take** a big risk and go to bed dirty. "I'm very nervous about this," he **said to** himself, "but I must try. I wish it weren't so hard!"

Meanwhile, Farmer Brown rushed into the stable. "I'd better saddle up quickly and round up the animals that are still out in this terrible storm," he said. "Come on, Biscuit, don't let me down."

The farmer snapped at the reins, and Biscuit knew what he had to do. "I can't waste any time tapping and blinking," he sighed. "There are lives in danger!" So he took a deep breath and moved forward and was soon galloping along at a fast pace.

In the beginning, he was nervous that Farmer Brown was going to fall off him and break his neck. But eventually he gained confidence, and by the time he was back in his stall, he felt really good, because for the first time he did what he knew was right, not what O. C. Flea had told him to do.

By the next morning, the storm had passed, and the sun was shining brightly in a clear blue sky. It was a brighter day for many of the animals on the farm, too. Henrietta awoke and realized that nothing had happened to the coop, even though she hadn't followed any of O. C. Flea's directions. As the day wore on, Henrietta found that she was thinking less and less about lining up her chicken feed, checking her eggs, or grooming her feathers. This left her lots of time for fun.

Biscuit was given a hero's treatment for saving the animals. The farmer gave him an extra-long grooming and lots of sugar cubes. His friend Trotter was proud of him.

Inside the barn, Maybelle smiled. "You did a really good job, Daisy. You saved lots of the milk."

"But I'm still a little worried," Daisy admitted. "Did you see if I drooled in the milk?"

Maybelle almost answered her but thought a moment, then said, "Maybe you'll be better off if I don't answer the questions that dumb flea gets you to ask. So from now on, I won't!"

At first, Daisy would still ask the questions, but Maybelle ignored
her, and eventually, Daisy stopped asking.

"This is strange," Daisy said. "When you don't answer my questions,
I feel as if I don't have to ask them anymore. I feel less worried."

After making this discovery, Daisy tried hard not to ask the questions, and she let the farmer milk her with much less fuss. The other cows began to talk to her, and she felt more a part of everything.

Snort continued to try hard to ignore O. C. Flea. But he wanted to understand better what had happened to him. Trotter suggested that he talk to the barn owl, who seemed to understand the problem.

"Hoot," said Snort, "tell me about O. C. Flea."

The owl pulled out a zoological encyclopedia. Under the entry for O. C. Flea it read, "Obsessive-Compulsive (O. C.) Flea. A sneaky, mischievous insect that spreads lies and causes obsessions or upsetting thoughts to repeat in the heads of its victims over and over again. Victim may also have compulsions—bad habits, such as washing hands many times, tapping feet, or asking the same questions over and over."

"How do you stop O. C. Flea?" he asked the owl.

"It says it here, under TREATMENTS:

"**Treatment 1.** A behavior zootherapist can give the animal new tools that will make that animal less afraid of his or her thoughts. The therapist helps the animal fight the strange and annoying habits.

"**Treatment 2.** Sometimes it is too hard to fight it, and the animal may be sent to a zoodoctor, who gives him or her special medication. The medication and what they've learned in the therapy together will definitely help the more difficult cases.

"**WARNING:** Don't forget that even when the treatment helps, O. C. Flea will come back every time there is an opportunity. Animals that are feeling badly because of things happening at school or at home are at special risk. Sometimes animals simply grow too tired of fighting O. C. Flea, and that makes them an easy catch again.

Snort realized that by chance the storm had helped all of the troubled animals on the farm get a little better. He was amazed, too, at how small O. C. Flea seemed now, and how much bigger he had seemed when he was convincing Snort to do strange things. But although he felt much more confident, he knew that O. C. Flea would come back, so they all needed to learn how to fight him.

Snort decided to post a big sign with O. C. Flea's picture. The sign read:

The story of Farmer Brown's farm and O. C. Flea spread far and wide. Children who heard it and were worried about their thoughts told their parents about it and about any habits they had that were upsetting them.

One boy, Ben, admitted that he had been very embarrassed by his thoughts and actions and had kept them to himself. But after hearing the story, he told his parents, and together they found a therapist to help him. At the therapist's, he learned all about OCD, or *obsessive-compulsive disorder*. He did some special exercises that helped to change his behaviors, a little like the storm in the story changed the animals' behaviors. The exercises were called *exposure* and *response prevention*.

Like for the animals, it was very hard for Ben at first. But the more Ben practiced, the better he felt. Now, instead of telling people that he's a kid with OCD, he tells them he's a kid who's O. C. Free!

About the Author

E. Katia Moritz, Ph.D., received her first degree as a psychologist at the Catholic University of Rio de Janeiro, Brazil. She moved to New York in 1991, to work as a visiting professional at the Albert Ellis Institute. Pursuing her interest in obsessive-compulsive disorder, she later joined the Institute for Bio-behavioral Therapy and Research in Great Neck, New York. Her research in the area of childhood OCD led to the development of manualized treatment programs using innovative approaches. In conjunction with this work, she received her Ph.D. in clinical and school psychology from Hofstra University, Hempstead, New York. Dr. Moritz is currently a psychology resident at the Miami Children's Hospital Dan Marino Center and is involved in the development of an OCD program for children there.